T0078077

Is Every Cab Driver Called Roger?

Mounira Chaieb

Langaa Research & Publishing CIG
Mankon, Bamenda

Publisher:
Langaa RPCIG
Langaa Research & Publishing Common Initiative Group
P.O. Box 902 Mankon
Bamenda
North West Region
Cameroon
Langaagrp@gmail.com
www.langaa-rpcig.net

Distributed in and outside N. America by African Books Collective
orders@africanbookscollective.com
www.africanbookscollective.com

ISBN-10: 9956-551-33-3

ISBN-13: 978-9956-551-33-0

About this Book

This is a book of anecdotes – a product of my reflections on both my personal and professional life as a young Tunisian female journalist, coming to work for the 'largest broadcaster in the world' and live in the big city, that is London all by myself. This book traces the Tunisia I grew up in in the sixties – few years after it gained its independence from France, where my parents and I belonged to very different worlds. I come from a traditional family and society where a girl – no matter how educated – only leaves her parents' house to her husband's. So, for my family to allow me that, was something totally unheard of. The book highlights some of the most impressionable experiences I had while working in the Bush House offices in my home department; on secondment to other departments or on duty tours — work trips abroad for the BBC and other places. At some point and for many years, I was the only Tunisian in the whole organisation. This book also traces what I make of the changes that my country of origin has been through over the years, especially since 2011 and the beginning of what's referred to as 'The Arab Spring' that started there and spread like wildfire to other countries in the region. London is also the place where I met my late husband, the Pan-Africanist Dr Tajudeen Abdul-Raheem. We met by chance three times in three different places before we could speak and the rest as they say is history! I was probably the first Tunisian girl to marry a Nigerian. This book tackles the many challenges our union faced, the issue of identity for our two mixed-race daughters – something very rare back home – and for myself as a Tunisian – British or British-Tunisian, having spent longer in the UK than I did in Tunisia.

Mounira Chaieb was born in Tunis, Tunisia. She is a graduate of the University of Tunis, Faculty of Arts and Human Sciences in English Literature and Language. She was hired by the BBC World Service to work in its Arabic Department as a radio broadcast journalist essentially, so she moved to London in the summer of 1987.

She managed to work in various departments of the wider BBC: Arts and Features, The African Service in English and the Training Department.

She worked as Editor, Presenter, Producer, Reporter and Trainer until she left the BBC in 2011. Now, she works as a freelance journalist, mentor, writer and consultant among several other things.

She was married to the Pan -Africanist, the late Dr Tajudeen Abdul-Raheem. She lives in London with their two daughters.

Acknowledgements

To Aida and Ayesha, *mammou 'inayya*, my daughters who have always supported me especially in my writing. Thank you for always reminding me that not every story worth telling should be the subject of investigative journalism.

To my late mother, Fatma, who throughout her life always wished she had been able to read and write. In another lifetime, under different circumstances that would have allowed for an education, who knows how far this woman would have gone.

To my best friend, Alejandra, who has travelled the long road with me and has always been by my side.

And finally, to Tajudeen my late husband, who saw this work through its inception and remains so integral to some of the anecdotes given here.

Table of Contents

Foreword

I was born in Tunis, the bustling capital of Tunisia, into a humble home. The Tunisia I grew up in in the sixties was for the most part, a stable, progressive and forward-thinking country. This was in spite of the fact that only a few years earlier, Tunisia had just emerged out of the devastating colonial period, lasting seventy - five years and opening irreparable socioeconomic rifts across the country in its wake. The long-awaited emancipation from the colonial power yielded new hope for a better Tunisia.

Tunisia was headed at that time by the late Habib Bourguiba, our beloved President remembered most notably for ushering in the era of decolonisation, who made sincere efforts to equalise social conditions for the two sexes. He was a Sorbonne-alumni trained in law, and saw what was considered at the time the 'radical' value of enshrining women's rights into the new post-colonial constitution, as part of what he perceived would be Tunisia's rapid path towards modernisation. He spared no effort in implementing this. His main priorities primarily included the improvement of the country's educational system, fighting gender inequality on a legislative level, developing the economy, and maintaining a neutral foreign policy. Such measures made him an exception among Arab leaders.

Perhaps one of his most major reforms was the Code of Personal Status passed in 1956 – the year Tunisia became independent. The Code put forth a series of progressive, uniquely Tunisian laws aimed specifically at establishing equality between women and men on an institutional level, spanning a number of sectors. The complete abolition of polygamy, the creation of a judicial procedure for divorce and the criminalisation of forced marriage all outlined by the Code increased the visibility of women's rights, and made clear strides towards achieving equality. These steps were built upon by Bourguiba's successor, Zine El Abidine Ben Ali, when he came to power in 1987 in his July 1993 amendment. This amendment legalised the right of women to transfer citizenship to their children, in marriages with a non-Tunisian citizen. Until the amendment was passed, only men had held this right.

Education of both boys and girls was, in Bourguiba's view, a fundamental characteristic of a developed country. Bourguiba was known for paying in-person surprise visits to the rural areas in particular, where conservative attitudes towards gender were concentrated. These visits were carried out to check that not only boys were sent to school, but girls too. If he found any breaches, he would warn the fathers as the traditional heads of the household, that if they did not oblige by a fixed deadline, they would be punished severely by the state. This could result in a prison sentence.

My grandparents migrated from Sousse, a southeastern coastal city intermittently populated to a large extent by Tunisians from surrounding areas arriving in search of work. It was common for people to be frequently uprooting themselves from their hometowns, moving around strategically according to the harvest season, before finally settling in Tunis. My parents got married in the 1950s and had seven of us. Though they were both uneducated — my father had attended only a Koranic school — as a result, they abided by the law and sent all of us to school. Education at all levels was free then, and the standards were very good. Contrary to the norm of their generation, there was no longer any excuse not to get an education.

****

From the earliest days of my childhood, I was always a curious child. I seized upon absolutely anything I could learn. When I was told stories, I was always on the edge of my seat eagerly waiting to hear what happened next, and I would want to know every minute detail, until the person telling the story got fed up with the incessant questions and just rushed to the end. This early curiosity soon found its calling in languages, as the Francophone curriculum ensured that French was learned from the age of seven alongside Modern Standard Arabic, which any Arabic speaker can confirm is markedly different from regional dialects spoken in day to day life. I thoroughly enjoyed studying languages, and having French teachers at secondary school, followed by British lecturers later on at university; it all opened the door to a new world for me. Exposure to other cultures, especially in my comparably tiny, off-the-radar home country of Tunisia, only inflated my curiosity about the world.

In my third year of university, I spent three months in Canterbury in the South of England with a group of fellow students, a trip necessary in order to fulfil the requirements of our English Language and Literature degree. Part of the trip involved living in homestays with English families. It was my first time ever out of Tunisia and away from my family. That experience was a real discovery for me, as my first step towards independence. The whole trip left such an impression on me that upon my return home that autumn, I started frequenting the British Cultural Centre in Tunis to revise for my exams around twice or three times a week, to maintain my connection with the British culture. In retrospect, it comes as no surprise that I later ended up working and living in the UK.

Besides languages, I also had an early fascination with radio. I found it absolutely magical. As I explain in detail later on, this love of radio was my late father's influence, but this lasting influence has survived the test of time. I still prefer radio to any other medium, and always tune in from the moment I wake up, keeping it on in the background all day. For me, radio is the most powerful medium because it draws a picture for the listeners in words and sounds instead of presenting it visually to them. It requires a great deal of storytelling and invites the listener's imagination to participate.

****

From a very young age, I witnessed so many injustices and malpractices in my society against the most vulnerable groups: women and girls, disabled folk, the poor and working-class of Tunisia. And these were just groups that were *visibly* marginalized, openly harassed, bullied, ridiculed, humiliated and discriminated against and very few people questioned these practices, but got nowhere. As for members of the LGBT+ community for example, they were rendered completely invisible in mainstream society because of the religious and cultural taboos surrounding non-heteronormative sexualities. I grew up silently wishing that I could find the power to address these issues. So, when I finally became a radio journalist, I seized every opportunity to raise awareness and sought to change misperceptions and sexist practices mainly within the Arab World. Given all this, did I become a journalist by chance? I don't think so.

When I first joined the BBC, we worked according to a shift-based pattern: a ten-day cycle, rotating four-day shifts, two nights and three days off (with the day before the first night shift considered a working day). Every newcomer was required to do this unless they had valid health reasons and a corresponding medical report to prove that they could not work according to this schedule.

Night shifts could be especially brutal, and as they constituted a big chunk of my shifts over the 24-year span of my time at the BBC, my sporadic sleeping pattern never recovered. The only upshot of this was that you ended up working with the same colleagues over a period of time, so you got to know them as people, outside of the work context. Bush House, the previous Strand headquarters of the BBC World Service in central London (now moved to Oxford Street in the heart of the Capital), was quiet at night and the pace of work was generally slower, save for the periods of mass conflict erupting across the Arab Peninsula, where we worked tirelessly through the night to keep up to date with the ever-changing developments. The usually-subdued mood of the night shift thus presented us with plenty of opportunity to make real friendships, keeping each other going through the night with multiple trips to the canteen to load up on caffeine for the long night ahead.

The canteen on the lower ground was like the United Nations of the BBC, where we met colleagues from almost every corner of the globe, who like us, were broadcasting to their own countries and regions in their own languages. The cooks themselves came from all parts of the world, and we soon got to know them by name. In return they would remember who was who according to dietary and religious preferences. The main newsroom on the fourth floor of the South Eastern block of the building was another lively meeting place, where translators from various language services would meet their individual English editors of the news bulletin and translate the bulletin together. Newsreaders would join later and go through the bulletin point by point before heading to the studios. Our shift pattern as radio journalists in the Arabic Service was almost identical to that of these neighbouring colleagues. As for us at the Arabic Service on the fourth floor of Centre block, we would get each other warm food at dawn after transmission, or bring some homemade food to share. It was, among other things, a way to maintain cultural connections with our fellow Arabs.

****

Over the course of my career, I thoroughly enjoyed working on programmes and documentaries, much more than the news and current affairs. I found the news quite repetitive and especially in the case of the Arab World, very depressing. Although they were undoubtedly important, reporting on those stories — especially as a North African for whom these went far beyond the studio — definitely took their toll after a while. It was also difficult to achieve the same impact with news stories that soon came to resemble one another. Documentaries by comparison had more scope for creativity and impact. Many of the documentaries I worked on involved getting out of the office and interviewing real people about real issues — something I always looked forward to.

Through these documentaries I tackled all kinds of issues, from those related to the *Arab Spring, human rights in the Arab World, the War on Terror*, issues and perceptions around *Muslims in Europe, illegal African immigration*, issues faced by young people and the status of disabled people in the Arab World. Some of my work included issues that are considered taboo in Arab countries even in today, such as honour killings, female circumcision, drug use, sex education and much more. To help get a range of perspectives on these series, I interviewed all kinds of people: heads of states, ministers, high-profile politicians, opposition figures, UN High Commissioners for Refugees and Human Rights, specialists in different areas, artists, writers, sportspeople and laywomen and men. Working with so many different people from all walks of life always offered the opportunity to break new ground.

This book highlights some of the most impressionable experiences I had while working in the *Bush House* offices in my home department; on secondment to other departments or on duty tours — work trips abroad for the BBC and other institutions— as well as what I make of the changes that my country of origin witnessed the year I left the BBC.

These anecdotes are a product of my reflections on both my personal and professional life.

Chapter 1

The Early Days

I grew up in Tunisia's transitional era of decolonisation, in a working-class area on the outskirts of the capital, Tunis, in a small neighbourhood called *Cité Zouhour*. The history of the neighbourhood had started with *Cité Zouhour 1 and 2*: areas distinguished by blocks of flats built by the government – the equivalent of council flats in the UK — and let out at affordable rent. Our neighbourhood was *Cité Zouhour 3*, and was much less organised by comparison: most houses had been built without the local council's permission, and the roads were largely unpaved which meant that when it rained, the area was very muddy. It took about fifteen minutes to walk from the house where we lived to the main road, and its scattering of shops and buildings. My primary school was even further away.

There were two tall palm trees at the beginning of our narrow street, which we would take shelter under on particularly hot days and as kids, we imagined had ghosts inside that would show up at night. There was a salt – lake south of our area, where we played during our summer holidays. A man we nicknamed the *'Algerian'* as anyone non-Tunisian immediately became distinguishable to us for this, had a French-style house and a farm close by, where he grew wheat. He had a few animals on the farm: a horse, a handful of cows, and a dog and we got chased and cursed by him many times for daring to come so close to his farm.

Eventually a *Cité Zouhour 4 and 5* was constructed. These expansions reflected the movement of the time as more and more people from poorer parts of the country moved into the capital looking for work, just as my grandparents had done so before them. Almost the entirety of my extended family was packed into *Cité Zouhour 3*; all of my uncles, aunties and cousins lived next door to us or opposite the narrow streets from one another.

Cité Zouhour, *Tunis where I grew up*

****

When I joined the BBC, I was in my mid-twenties, and the only place I had visited outside of my home country of Tunisia was Canterbury the cosy, quiet city known for its proud cathedral and rolling green hills, situated south in the UK. I had visited two years earlier in 1985 as part of an exchange training programme between Kent's Christ Church University and my own place of study, the University of Tunis. The general expectation of me undertaking a degree programme in English Literature and Language was that I would go on to become a teacher of the English language, and the programme had been designed specifically with that pathway in mind.

With my university group and one of our teachers, Monsieur Mohammed Trabelsi in Canterbury, Kent in 1985

Contrary to convention however, I was always plagued with a vague certainty that I would not become a teacher. The source of this certainty is something I have never been able to identify, but I have often wondered if it had anything to do with how badly behaved some of the students around me were as I was growing up, and whether the possibility of being put to task with attempting to regain control over an unruly class seemed far too daunting a job for someone as mild-natured and introverted as myself.

Rather than choosing my area of study for its most viable career prospects, I had instead chosen a language-oriented degree simply because I had a natural love of languages. As a young girl I readily devoured any books I could get my hands on, which were often whatever my elder sister had brought home from her secondary school library that week. French was introduced into the curriculum in the second year of primary school, and studying it brought with it all the lustre of a new language and culture. So, my siblings and I would read books in both Arabic and French and dream elaborately of the sophisticated lifestyles depicted in Beirut, the elegant wide avenues of Paris, the old town of Cairo overflowing with people… all places so far away from our home in tiny Tunis.

Among some of the great names we grew up reading were *Mikhael N'aima* and *Jubran Khalil Jubran* from Lebanon; *Ghada Al-Samman* from Syria, *Taha Hussain, Tawfiq El Hakim* and *Naguib Mahfouz* from Egypt; *Victor Hugo, Voltaire* and *Jean Jacques* Rousseau from France. Through their eyes, it felt as though we could see the world.

When it came to choosing a language degree, the decision had been intuitive based on my love for the subject. But my decision later in life to pursue a radio journalism career in particular, as opposed to television or print, I attribute completely to the early influence of my late father. He was a taxi driver. Every day, when he came home from work, he would collapse on the old green chaise and when it was hot on a mat on the floor of our living room and flick through his small transistor radio. He was always listening to the news on stations that came from places across the diaspora: Monte Carlo from France, Radio Orient from Egypt, several Libyan radio stations (the names of which memory betrays now).

BBC Arabic was broadcasting to the whole of the Maghreb on short wave at the time. So, if my father was lucky enough to catch a frequency, it was by mere chance and it wouldn't be long before it became muffled, riddled with static and eventually disappear. Even then, the voices that came all the way from London to Francophone Tunisia left a huge impact on me. I could never have dreamed that the day would come when the people from whom those voices came would eventually become my colleagues.

****

I often frequented the British Cultural Centre, that was part of the British Consulate located in the heart of Tunis to revise for my university exams as it offered a good-sized library, an expansive and quiet study area and of course, plenty of books and magazines. During my third and penultimate year at university, while at the Centre one afternoon I happened upon a copy of *Huna London*, the magazine produced internationally by the BBC Arabic Service. Flicking through on my way home, I saw an advert for Broadcast Assistants — the title the BBC World Service attached to its journalists in the '80s and '90s. The position was based in London and the main requirement was proficiency in both English and Arabic. It seemed like the perfect job for my young self, restless to get out into the world and put my love for languages to the test.

Within a few days, my application was filled and well on its way to London. It was only after sending it off that imposter syndrome reared its ugly head and I started doubting my decision: What if they were looking for experienced journalists and turned me down? On the other hand, what if I *was* selected and required to go to London while I still had a degree to finish? The latter question posed an even bigger dilemma.

Months passed and I carried on with my university studies, almost forgetting about the application entirely, until one autumn day I received a letter informing me that a BBC team would be in Tunis in March 1987. I had been invited to take part in a written test and an interview. In spite of my nervousness and feelings of inadequacy, I reasoned that pulling out at this stage would be a wasted opportunity no matter the outcome. So, I confirmed that I would be attending.

Thanks to a series of reforms, Tunisia's post-independence President, *Habib Bourguiba*, had ensured that university education remained free for all, and students also received a monthly allowance to cover living costs. It was a great source of personal achievement and pride for me to able to manage my own finances in this way as my family came from small means, and my hope was to be able to support myself and eventually support them too. With the money from my allowance I bought a brand-new outfit for my first ever job interview. I had absolutely no idea what to expect or who to talk to beforehand for advice. But I prepared by reading English newspapers and listening to news as much as I could, entirely in English. I remember finding the written test really tough, but I answered as much as I could. In the interview, I was just myself; no retouches.

Soon after the interview, final exams came around the corner and I became totally preoccupied with exam preparation. I didn't have any time to spend deliberating about the interview and whether or not I had been accepted. A reminder of the whole process only came one summer day in June, at the height of exam season, when my younger brother, Faouzi, came running home and breathlessly announced, *'Mounira, you have a letter from London!'*

My family had known about my application and the test. My mother was already both worried and saddened by the mere possibility of me leaving home to work and live in London, which in spite of it being only two and a half hours away on a plane, felt so distant from us all. So, when the letter finally arrived, her face was wrangled with worry as she waited for me to confirm my fate. My six siblings by comparison were extremely intrigued and excited. At this point, I was shaking with nerves. With trembling hands, I opened the official-looking, baby blue envelope with its distinctive *Par Avion* sticker on it and read through. I looked up and found the faces of my family all lit up with anticipation, with my mother's face markedly more apprehensive than the rest. In disbelief, I paused and with a big smile, announced that I had been selected! Everyone ran to me congratulating me with hugs and cheers except my mother, who in her grief at the prospect of her young daughter moving overseas, turned and walked away. I tried to comfort and reassure her that I would always call and visit and, above everything else, help her financially. She only managed half a smile as she was still not very comforted by the looming idea of it all. I hoped and trusted that in time, she would come to see the value of such a rare opportunity and that it would bring the financial relief my family needed.

I wrote to the BBC thanking them and explaining that I was waiting for my final university exam results before I could join the company. They were very accommodating and said I could go whenever I was ready. All the doubts and fears that I had had about applying in the first place had in the end amounted to nothing. I was awarded a degree in English Language and Literature and joined BBC Arabic that same summer. I arrived in London on the last day of July in 1987, fresh from university for my first proper job as a BBC journalist. Though it was summertime, it was a bit chilly — nowhere near the hot summers I was used to at home where it could get to 40 degrees in Tunis! A female colleague met me at Heathrow Terminal Two to take me to the BBC hostel in Central London.

هل تفتح أوروبا أبوابها للهجرة؟!

يمثل حلقة اليوم من برنامج الراعي الأخر من هذا كل سكن العربية ان
الوطنية جان تكفل القادمين اليها من الدول النامية اذ تقبل المنطقة
تحفف اوروبا سياساتها الخاصة بالهجرة وتفتح
الاسلام جان تكفل القادمين اليها من بلد الي الي الاخر سواء عن اختيار او
اضطرار ان مصيرة الاندماس من اهناك نحو 150 مليون
منين اعلى من ابو ولت معنى لعقاب تشير الامم المتحدة من ان اوروبا
تحفف في ازمة ديمغرافية حادة خلال السنوات الخمسين المقبلة من
كبار السن من الاوروبيين يعيشون مدة
سكوانه اقتصاديتها فكبار السن لا يزال سن التقاعد في معظم
ان تؤثر على مستوى المعيشة بينما لا يزال سن التقاعد في معظم
المشيبين خمس بين الستين والخمس وستين سنة مما يعني بالتالي
الاوروبية يتراوح بين الستين والخمس والسؤال هو كيف تنفق
العاملة في انخفاض شديد. والسؤال هو كيف تنفق
لايدي في مستوياتها الحالية دون اللجوء الي ايد عاما
اقتصادياتها المزدهرة في

البرنامج وتقدمه منيرة الشايب ويذاع اليوم الاحد الساعة السا
تعد ودقيقتين مساء، ويعاد الساعة الحادية عشرة وخمس بقا
سف ودقيقتين مساء، ويعاد الساعة الواحدة والنصف وثماني دقائق بعد ظهر الثلا
اح الاثنين، والساعة الواحدة والنصف وثماني دقائق بعد ظهر الثلا
ة وعشر دقائق بعد ظهر الخميس بتوقيت جرينتش.

In the BBC Arabic studio in the early years

****

My work experience prior to the BBC consisted solely of a summer job during my university years as a translator, working with material from English into French and Arabic and vice versa. At the time of joining the BBC, I was in my mid-twenties, which probably made me the youngest member of staff. An older Tunisian compatriot joined around the same time I did. She was already a journalist in Tunisia but her contract with the BBC came to end and she went back home. Another male colleague joined years later, but he also left after a few years. I was the only Tunisian within the whole company for years after that!

The fact that my family allowed me — however reluctantly — to leave for Europe by myself at my young age, has always been a source of controversy for those to whom I tell this story. The effect is always compounded by the fact that I am not even the eldest of my siblings; of my four brothers, two were older than me, and of my two sisters, I was the middle child. Traditionally it is not the usual thing in many Arab societies, even to the present day, for a young daughter to leave the family unit without being married first. Custom dictates that the 'honour' of the family is bestowed onto its female members and as a result, women are restricted in their choices and decisions. Many freedoms, such as the will to start a career overseas, can be interpreted as going against convention. The deeply patriarchal nature of many Arab societies gives the men of the family complete authority over the women's behaviour and choices as any 'dishonourable' act would bring into question their manhood, which is of utmost importance. In fact, a brother – not necessarily the father - can decide to stop his sister from going to school if he thought it was going to attract gossip and that was totally acceptable. The most absurd thing I grew up witnessing was the expectation that a girl – no matter how old she was – could not go anywhere except to school, without being accompanied by a male member of the family mostly a brother, even if he was just a little boy and the age gap up to twenty years!

Within my family, my mother felt the pressure of convention more than all of my aunties because it was only me and my two sisters in our extended family who had made it all the way to university. Such a notable achievement also meant that we were under the watchful eyes of our whole family, waiting for a seemingly harmless 'mistake' to be made on our part that would bring on the inevitable dishonour, and with it, gossip and scorn from the extended family. These mistakes could be anything, from getting caught talking to a male schoolmate in public, laughing with female friends or even just getting home later than usual, which happened often because the buses were always packed. So, you can imagine the kind of immense pressure that we the girls, felt.

My parents and I inhabited two very different worlds. My mother and the consternation she felt at my departure were emblematic of the oppressive society in which she grew up, where women especially, were deprived of any education. A number of unfortunate incidents at school could have been avoided if my mother had some degree of education! She was very intelligent, a quick learner and regretted not being educated, not her choice or decision though. During secondary school when I was revising out loud for my exams, my mother always could memorise everything whether it was literature, history or languages that involved words from French and helped me whenever I forgot something. She could pick up words from French and Italian languages even if she only heard them once as if she was learning them for years! But my mother was born in the 1930s when Tunisia was under French colonial rule and education of girls was not common.

Since independence in 1956, Tunisian women have benefitted from the right to education, equal pay, opportunities to travel freely and the right to file for divorce. In the present day, there is much contention surrounding a recent bill introduced by the late President *Beji Caid Essebsi* in 2018 to give equal inheritance rights to women. The move has been applauded by some both domestically and abroad as a step in the right direction. To others however, this bill, together with Bourguiba's historic criminalization of polygamy the same year Tunisia gained its independence, has garnered much criticism from other Arab countries, with people even calling these laws un-Islamic. It was important for Bourguiba that the country he led was secular, where politics were separate from religion and where religion was an individual matter.

So, I was growing up at a time when convention as we knew and understood it was being broken by the state, and the future of Tunisia's socioeconomic landscape was being mapped out by a radical President. I was eager to leap into this new world and make use of all the opportunities it had to offer, even if it wasn't always the 'approved' thing to do.

Chapter 2

The Journey

Bush House, home of the BBC World Service until 2008

'*Moo-nee-ra Shay-ebb, yes?*' I corrected overly emphatically, familiar with the mispronunciation. Apparently, the pronunciation of my name had been a source of difficulty for almost everyone I had met in the UK so far.

'*It's your cab driver, miss, and I'm outside.*' He confirmed.

'*Thank you, sir, I will be out in two minutes.*'

And so, ensued the nightly ritual that commenced at around 10pm, where a taxi was sent by the BBC to drop me off promptly by 11pm at Bush House for the night shift.

Night after night, week after week, the telephone would ring promptly by 10pm signalling the arrival of the driver that evening. I would stifle laughter as yet another unfamiliar variant of what I had previously considered to be a very simple name to pronounce would bubble up through the speaker, and then I would voyage into the night to start work as seemingly the rest of the world around me prepared for sleep.

Night shifts were also great fun as there were always funny incidents, like this one:

'*Is every cab driver in London called Roger?*' The question tumbled hesitantly out of my mouth from the backseat of a cab or taxi that the BBC transport department used to arrange and pay for, en route to the night shift. I couldn't stop myself from asking, as I had heard cab drivers saying '*Roger*' at the end of every office call. To my surprise, the question was met with an outburst of laughter from the front seat. The taxi driver, not quite believing his ears paused before answering. '*No, that's our way of saying over to you!*'. Why Roger not any other name, I still wondered.

There were always funny incidents on and off air. One night - shift, a colleague was reading a political report from the BBC correspondent in Nigeria. The BBC correspondents sent their reports, known as 'dispatches' to us in English and we would translate them into Arabic. I was the producer of the news programmes of the dawn shift. As a producer, my place was always outside the cubicle of the presenter and the broadcasting team and next to the studio manager, now known as the technician, to guide them through the programme. This was because studio managers were mostly English-speakers and did not speak Arabic.

The report we were delivering involved *Ibrahim Babangida*, the Nigerian President at the time who annulled the June 12 1993. Before we went on air, my colleague asked me how to pronounce his name. I called the BBC Hausa service to confirm with them, as the President was a Hausa man, and got the correct pronunciation, following standard protocol when we were unsure (we often received calls from producers of other departments to confirm the pronunciation of Arabic names too). They told me the emphasis was on the 'ban' part of his name. But my colleague kept putting the emphasis on the 'gin', prolonging it every time to sound something like *Baba-gin-da*. I tried enunciating it to him the way my colleagues in the Hausa Service had said it, and after a few tries, he seemed to have mastered it. When he was on air however, it was a different story. He read the report with his usual professionalism, up until he reached the President's name and disastrously stumbled on it one attempt after another, which resulted in a laughing fit lasting something like ten seconds or so. In broadcasting time, ten seconds is a long while for a journalist to be laughing on air or even silent!

On another occasion, I went to the women's dormitory on the lower ground floor to get some rest before the beginning of my shift. This is something we all did fairly regularly as the process of acclimatising to sleeping during the daytime often left me sleep deprived. I could hardly sleep because there was always a lot of movement outside the doors of the dormitory with people going back and forth and I found it difficult adjusting to a different bed every time. So, I was used to giving up on the prospect of sleep altogether, and instead just closing my eyes for some time, or reading.

That night, I was particularly tired and desperately needed to rest. I tried frustratingly for something like thirty minutes to will myself to sleep, but was unsuccessful. The reason for my restlessness this time was because of someone snoring in intermittent, violent eruptions in one of the cubicles down the corridor. I turned and tossed, put my hands over my ears, and tried in every way I could to tune out. Nothing worked. So, with resignation I decided to get up, wash my face, get myself a tea from the canteen and head to the office on the fourth floor instead. I figured I would listen to the news and read a little, to regain some energy before the start of my shift.

As soon as I got in and switched on the light, I jumped with fear as I noticed some movement from under the desk I shared with other members of the team. I paused at the threshold of the door, squinting to try and make out what it was. I waited a little until the thing in question started moving again slowly. I got even more scared and almost screamed and ran away when, to my surprise, a person materialised out of the darkness under the desk. He rubbed his eyes, murmuring an embarrassed apology. Now that my eyes had adjusted, I recognised the familiar face of a male colleague of mine. He was lying flat under the desk, on the carpeted floor with no cover. In spite of his visible embarrassment he looked very tired, and explained that he had decided to sleep there because he had encountered the same problem in the men's dormitory, located at the beginning of the corridor before the women's, and hadn't slept because of someone's incessant snoring. I wondered if he was hearing the same rumbling snoring from the women's dormitory through the thick walls!

****

The excitement of coming to live in the bustling cosmopolitan city of London never wore off, but it also came with a few surprises upon my arrival. In addition to practicalities in Britain being markedly different from the rest of the world (driving on the right instead of the left, measuring in miles instead of kilometres, or feet and inches instead of meters and centimetres), one of the biggest culture shocks I encountered was the comparably unrestricted relations between men and women. How markedly different they were here compared to back home! It was quite a discovery to learn that it was perfectly normal and acceptable for young people to date freely and openly.

As I was setting up with the Studio Manager one Monday for a news programme, he asked me how my weekend had gone. I told him that I had done what I usually did on the weekends: rested mostly, squeezing in some time to catch a film at the cinema and clean the flat in preparation for the following week. When I returned the question, he answered that his sister had come home with her boyfriend for a family visit. He said it so matter-of-factly, but to me back then, young Tunisian girl that I was coming from a place where boyfriends were absolutely not allowed, and if I were to have one, he would be a huge secret kept from virtually everyone I knew — most especially my brothers — I was aghast. The culture shock reverberated once more as he confirmed that his sister and her boyfriend had slept in the same bed under the parental roof! I genuinely couldn't believe it that I asked him if he was Ok with that. He looked at me and said 'of course'!

I was also surprised to find that the English literature I had studied at university had no place in the modern English language. I discovered that Shakespearean English had been put to rest a long time ago, though until arriving in London I had been under the impression that that was the only English people spoke. My astonishment was compounded when I learned that some parts of London even had what sounded to me as their own language, known as a 'cockney' dialect. Cockney transformed the word 'paper' into 'piper'; a 'fiver' indicated 'five pounds'. It was very hard for me to understand it, or even find any connection between cockney English and the English I had been taught. Cockney even had special rhyming phrases that were supposed to mean something. 'Bread and cheese' combined became 'sneeze'. Or a 'Joanna' was a 'piano', as it was pronounced 'pee-anna' in Cockney. The list of words that were unrecognisable to me only grew longer over time.

Cockney aside, the one phrase that took me almost a year to decipher was the announcement by the conductor on some of London's tube stations to 'mind the gap'. This phrase has become synonymous with London over the years like Big Ben, Trafalgar Square, Mme Tussauds, the London Eye etc. The London Transport Authority must have realized in recent years the confusion the announcement has been causing to many people especially those new in the city and has made the announcement to say, 'Mind the gap between the train and the platform'. What a relief! I wasn't the only one who couldn't tell which gap.

I was even more shocked to learn that hardly anyone I met in the UK knew where Tunisia was. Upon hearing that I was from Tunisia, I was often asked if I meant Tanzania, which I was prepared to forgive on account of the similarities between the names and the fact that they are both in the same continent. When people asked if I meant Indonesia however, I was too shocked to even answer. I was perplexed that a country so geographically close and a well-known tourist destination remained so foreign to so many.

I have also met people in London from all corners of the globe, including places that I only knew existed on the map and even small islands that I never heard of before, especially in the Caribbean. I even built strong friendships with people from far away countries such as Uruguay, Bhutan, Myanmar, India, Bulgaria and many more.

As for my name, I spelt it slowly and wrote it down phonetically on so many occasions, for so many people... but very few were actually able to pronounce it correctly. I was called every M-name under the sun from Monica to Moira and Marina— my elderly English neighbour has decided that my name is Leena (no relationship whatsoever) and it took a while to realise she was actually calling me— but I was hardly ever called Mounira, the name my mother gave me.

Chapter 3

Homelessness Here and Back Home

The first thing that struck me about London was the sheer number of homeless people on the streets – something that I never witnessed in Tunis when I was growing up. Tunisia was and still is a developing country, considered part of the Global South, but 1970s and 80s Tunisia saw very few people sleeping rough, and beggars confined only to the larger cities, where they were few in number. That isn't to say that homelessness didn't exist in Tunisia: it could be that it did exist but people found shelter with family members, neighbours or mosques. Also, at the time the state adopted a welfare system and helped the poor and needy.

The long road between Holborn tube exit and Bush House, the BBC World Service building, was lined with theatres, banks, shops and restaurants. It was also home to many homeless people of all ages; men and women who would arrive in the early hours of the evening, particularly when it was cold and rainy. They would come with their beddings — a piece of cardboard and an old blanket or a stained white duvet. Each person would take their position at the entrance of a closed office or a bank before anyone else arrived to compete with them over the tiny space.

I saw various people reading books under streetlight, others listening to music on their Walkman (a small pocket size device where you played your cassette from, before MP3 and MP4 and definitely before smart devices), some people sat with their dogs. Soon enough I began to notice one disarming young man in particular with tattooed arms and shoulders asking young women specifically for money by sweet-talking them and flirting as they walked by. His charm and allure seemed to work well as I often saw a woman or two giving graciously!

One evening, I witnessed a big argument between one man and two others during which the former angrily threw away their cardboard, insisting that the spot was his and his alone as he ripped up the cardboard and shouted at them to go to hell, as if he had a rent contract with a landlord. The other two pleaded with him to let them spend the night, but the former was adamant. I remember walking away wondering whether it was the survival instinct or general anger with society and its cruelty that had made him act that way.

Years later as technology developed, I saw a middle-aged homeless man outside a bank in the same area wrapped up in his blanket and holding an iPad. The thought struck me immediately that anyone who could afford an iPad back home in Tunisia would be considered well-off. Homelessness where I came from resembled people in torn and dirty clothes begging on the street, unable to afford the most basic of needs. London introduced me to new standards of poverty and homelessness; I realized that here, not everything is as it seems. Someone could own a brand new (at the time) piece of technology and yet still not have a place to call home.

عالم المشردين ...

○ بقلم: منيرة الشايب

هل هي نزعة التملك، ام هي نقمة على المجتمع؟

سؤال طرحته على نفسي، مساء يوم من الأيام وأنا في طريقي الى العمل الليلي، فالشارع الذي يربط بين الاذاعة ومحطة المترو كثيرا ما يكون مزدحما بالمشردين الذين يلوذون اليه منذ ساعات المساء الأولى خاصة اذا كان الطقس ممطرا أو باردا، فالكل يحمل معه ما يشبه فراشا وهو عبارة عن قطعة كرتون (أو الورق السميك) وغطاءا باليا لياخذ مكانه امام مداخل المكاتب أو الشركات أو البنوك، قبل ان ينافسه عليه شخص اخر.

وقد شاهدت أشياء كثيرة اثناء مروري يوميا من ذلك الشارع، رأيت من يستمع الموسيقى من اجهزة الاستماع الخاصة walkman، والبرد يكاد يقطع ضلوعه، ورأيت من يحاول تثقيف نفسه فامسك كتابا مستعينا بانوار الشارع، ورأيت من حمل معه كلبه ليشاركه في بعض الدفء، ورأيت شابا وسيما ظهرت على كتفيه وذراعيه رسوم مختلفة من الوشم الذي أصبح موضة في الغرب يدفع عليها الشباب من الجنسين بينما بدأت هذه العادة تندثر في المجتمعات الشرقية باعتبار انها دليل تخلف.

وكان ذلك الشاب لايستجدي سوى الفتيات أو النساء الشابات باستخدام عبارات غاية في الرقة، ورأيت من تغدق عليه اموالا طائلة!!، وما إلى ذلك من المشاهد الكثيرة والمتعددة.

ولكن في ذلك المساء، شاهدت احدهم وقد وقف في منتصف الشارع وهو يصرخ غربوا من هنا، وكان بجانبه اثنان من زملائه ولدى اقترابي منهم، شاهدت ذلك الرجل وهو يرمي بالكرتون الذي يملكه الرجلان الاخران جانبا، ويقول وقد استشاط غضبا: هذا المكان لي، لا أريد أن اراكما في هذا المكان!! ثم لخص ذلك بعبارة: اذهبا الى الجحيم!!، بينما وقف الاخران وهما يتوسلان اليه ان يسمح لهما بقضاء تلك الليلة فقط، ولكنه رفض.

واصلت طريقي وأنا اتساءل هل ما فعله ذلك الرجل نابع من غريزة موجودة في كل انسان مهما كانت درجة فقره أو غناه، وتجعله يعتني بممتلكاته ويقاتل من اجل الدفاع عنها، ام انه نابع من نقمة على المجتمع الذي نشأ فيه ذلك الرجل وترعرع، وخدم ذلك المجتمع في احدى فترات حياته. ولكنه لفظه كما تلفظ النواة لانه لم يتمكن من الانصهار فيه لانه مجتمع يعظم الغني ويسحق الفقير.●

* من قسم البرامج الاخبارية

An article I wrote for Huna London, the magazine issued by the BBC Arabic Service on homelessness in London shortly after joining.

Chapter 4

Duty Tours

Tiny State

In October of 1994, I went on a duty tour or work trip to Kuwait.

The country's capital, Kuwait City, was comprised of just one long street lined with all the shops and banks and clinics one might need. I stayed in a well-known hotel – part of an international chain, opposite which sat a pharmacy. I needed medication for a sudden bout of high temperature and thought to just walk the two - minute distance to the pharmacy across the street, but in the hotel lobby I was stopped in my tracks by the receptionist. Apparently, it was in my best interest to take a taxi instead for my own safety. I laughed off the idea; although I knew harassment in many Arab countries especially, could be rampant at the worst of times, I was certainly not going to take a taxi for a two - minute walk! It sounded preposterous. But upon exiting through the hotel doors, I could not believe what was happening around me: Men in their cars winking at me, which was soon followed with beeping their car horns, kerb crawling, and spontaneous U-turns in the middle of the busy road! The whole ordeal was so stressful that my body became overcome with sweat, and it wasn't just because of the temperature!

I noticed Asian women on the street, but those same men did not even notice their presence, which was puzzling. Later, I asked a Kuwaiti journalist friend of mine what that was about. She told me that in most cases those ladies were domestic workers and, due to issues of classism and colourism, Gulf men did not consider them feminine enough to harass!

A few days later, the Kuwaiti Ministry of Information arranged a trip for all of the foreign journalists to the Iraqi border. This was in the wake of the second Iraqi threat to invade again after the Gulf War of 1991 when Iraq did invade Kuwait and was pushed out by an international coalition. That military campaign was devastating to Iraq, but its late President then Saddam Hussain, was not deterred. The Ministry wanted to show us in concrete terms how tangible the Iraqi threat was. It was an area where Iraqi troops advanced towards the border and the Kuwaiti forces, backed by international support, were constantly pushing them back. It was there that I interviewed the British Defence Minister then, Malcom Rifkind who happened to be in the country on an official visit at the time.

When I heard the word 'border', I thought we were up for a very long journey, as country borders are not typically located anywhere close to the city centre, where we were staying. So, I packed up all my research papers in preparation (as these were the days of yesteryear where internet research was not something I could do, let alone conveniently carry on one portable cellular device). Next, I packed my recording equipment: an old - fashioned heavy recorder known as *marantz*, a microphone, a pair of headphones, spare batteries and a two - litre bottle of mineral water in my backpack.

As soon as we boarded the coach, I got my research material out and started to read through, prepared to spend the long journey brushing up on some necessary research. But before fifteen minutes had passed, the coach stopped, and everyone got up to leave. With my documents still on my lap, I looked up, confused. I thought perhaps there was an issue on the road or a technical fault with the coach. I asked a fellow journalist who had been sitting nearby why we had abruptly stopped and he replied simply, 'we are here.'

All my life, I had believed that Tunisia was a very small country. But to make it to the border by road with Algeria on the West or to Libya on the South, one would need between seven to ten hours at the very least. Before that, I had never visited any country so small that you can get to the border in less than twenty minutes! It felt like crossing into another country without realizing it.

Kuwait, October 1994

Kuwait, October 1994

Limousine

During my years at the BBC I was dispatched to various places around the world to cover all kinds of stories: political, social, religious… pretty much anything that was deemed relevant to the Arab world and the diaspora. On one such work trip for the BBC, or duty tour, as it was called at the time, I had been sent to Sweden to cover a conference titled *'Muslims in Europe'*, their integration in the societies they lived in and whether there was a need for more rapprochement and dialogue between the main religions of Europe. This trip was in the early autumn of 1995.

At a conference in 1995

Upon my arrival in Stockholm airport I had a comical exchange.

'Excuse me Sir, do you know where my taxi is?' I asked a man behind the information desk at the spotlessly clean airport after waiting for about twenty minutes. The man, stern-faced but polite, replied in perfect English, 'your taxi is outside, madam.' 'But I've just checked and I can't see it,' I responded, once again scanning the expensive-looking queue of cars lining up outside the airport. The man then pointed to a white limousine waiting by the kerb and said, to my great astonishment, '*that* is your taxi madam, and the driver has been waiting for you.' Immediately taken aback, I stammered an apologetic response 'I'm sorry, but I can't afford a limousine on the BBC allowance.'

This allowance was a sum of daily expenses based on the cost of living in individual countries we visited on our duty trips and covered mainly transport, food and work -related phone calls. We were supposed to keep receipts and fill forms when you got back to show how much we had spent.

The Swedish man behind the desk smiled a tiny, reassuring smile. 'It's alright, madam. Those are our taxis in Sweden. It will cost you the same as a normal taxi.' With excitement bubbling in my stomach, I walked towards this unbelievably luxurious car where the driver was waiting to take me on my very first limousine ride.

Do I want to be eaten y by crocodiles?

Fast forward four years to 1999, I had put forward a project idea to my editor for a series of radio documentaries on people with special physical needs within the Arab world: their status in society, how they were viewed with pity and or completely marginalized by society as a whole, how they were portrayed negatively by the media and how, with very few exceptions, there were virtually no laws to give them rights or make accessibility possible. The aim of the series was to deal with the issue from a human- rights perspective.

Upon its approval, one of the places I visited was Khartoum, Sudan. Before I arrived there, I was in transit at Cairo Airport where the following happened:

At the door of the ladies' restroom, a middle-aged Egyptian lady was handing out toilet tissue in exchange for money. Extending the toilet roll with one hand, she held her other hand out towards me, palm-up and expectant. 'Where's this beauty going to?', she asked. I knew she was probably not supposed to collect money for it, I also knew that she was just flattering me to get a tip or *bakshiish* as it's called in the Middle East. So, to humour her, I answered 'this beauty is going to Khartoum.' The woman's face immediately changed as alarm muddled her features. She beat her chest hard with her hand

and asked 'why do you want to go Sudan, my daughter? Do you want to be eaten by crocodiles?'

In Sudan, gathering material for the series on Disability in 1999

I did not reply, shook my head and walked away. But she followed me insisting that it was in my best interest not to go to Sudan and that she knew many people who had been there and saw crocodiles with their own eyes. I couldn't help but wonder if this woman seriously believed that crocodiles were roaming free on the streets of Khartoum. It seemed almost a joke, but the alarm and concern on her face were undoubtedly genuine.

As soon as I came back, I told the story to a dear colleague of mine from Sudan. I expected him to be offended, instead, he couldn't stop laughing and asked me to tell him the story again and again every time we saw each other. I think Sudanese people are used to some of the prejudices that their next-door neighbours hold about their country.

Sudan, 1999

I also think despite their geographical closeness, their common history, Pharaoh civilization consisting of Egypt, Sudan and Ethiopia and the fact the Egypt is actually in Africa, most Egyptians do not feel a connection with the continent. This is something common among North Africans that I will come back to in another chapter.

I also think that this has to do with Arab standards of beauty being: fair complexion, green or blue eyes, straight hair etc. Sudanese men have often been portrayed in Egyptian drama as domestic workers, subservient, lazy and not very intelligent, while their women as not attractive or desirable. Now, I wonder what the *Black Lives Matter* movement would make of those attitudes.

Sudan, 1999

Upon my return, the flight from Khartoum to Cairo was due to leave at around 7 am. I did not want to miss it, so before 5 am, I was already at the airport, checked in, went through security and waited to board the plane.

All flights came and went except mine. It was delayed by more than two hours. When it finally landed and we started to board, I asked a flight attendant about the reason for the delay. I was shocked when he said, 'take a look at the state of their (meaning the Sudanese) tarmac'. I said, 'what's wrong with it?'. 'Rotten and not good for any plane', was his reply. I said 'well, all flights came and left without a problem, why has *'their'* tarmac affected only your plane?' He looked at me sarcastically and said 'What brings you here anyway?

I wanted to tell him that actually I had the best five working days ever. I collected so much valuable material, interviewed so many interesting people, been taken to so many different places including a fascinating boat trip to where the white and blue Niles met and had no accident and certainly saw NO crocodiles!

Sudan, 1999, where the White and Blue Nile meet

Without a suitcase in Morocco

As part of the same project, I travelled to Morocco in the same year. I had already been there two years earlier to work on a groundbreaking documentary on illegal immigration from Africa to Europe via Spain. That trip, though it involved travelling between cities within Morocco and Spain, had gone smoothly and without any major hiccups but this more recent trip in 1999 by comparison, was somewhat a catastrophe.

I arrived in Morocco from Beirut, Lebanon. Thanks to the diligence of Beirut airport baggage handlers, my veteran olive green travelling suitcase — the sole survivor of many years of duty trips — had been broken beyond repair. So, I had to buy a new one. The newer model was an inexpensive thing in a rather elegant shade of green, but my loyalty to my old reliable bag made me feel a bit guilty about the new intruder. Nevertheless, I was too exhausted to spend much time on such sentimentalities. There was a flight to catch.

Duty tours required a lot of heavy baggage. This included my recording equipment and several kilograms' worth of documents. To make matters even more strenuous, the trip to Morocco was unnecessarily long, lasting longer than seven hours, and it was complicated above all: I had to travel to Paris first and wait there for about four hours, before I could catch a Royal Air Maroc flight to Rabat. A straight journey from London to Rabat would have been possible in no more than three hours. This circuitous flight was the product of the BBC's stringent requirements for the cheapest possible journey.

We arrived at Rabat Airport late on a Saturday evening. At the luggage collection point, I waited for my suitcase to be ejected onto the belt along with all of the other baggage from Paris. I watched with faltering hope as one by one, each of my fellow passengers hoisted their suitcases and exited through the double doors out of baggage claim until eventually I was the only one left. With one last shred of flimsy optimism I stood there waiting for my suitcase to suddenly burst through the conveyor belt. Unfortunately, this never came to be.

Defeated, I located the nearest airport official and asked him if all the luggage on the flight from Paris-Orly had arrived. He confirmed, very coldly, that it had. With this last shred of hope destroyed by his answer, I informed him of my predicament and couldn't help but start to cry. The unnecessarily long flight had robbed me of my ability to remain composed. The man examined me coldly. 'Why is a big woman like you crying like a child because of a suitcase?' Incensed by his insensitivity, I explained, 'because I'm not here on holiday, I'm here for work and if I can't have my suitcase then my work will be disrupted!' My visible anger seemed to kick something into gear as he then started a long process of enquiry about the suitcase (colour, size, content, etc.) and began halfheartedly filling out forms with my answers. Then he suggested that I go to my hotel to rest, and call again the following day. I felt this advice was delivered with the sole intention of getting rid of this bothersome, inexplicably emotional woman.

I cannot remember sleeping at all that night because my mind was completely fraught with worry about my upcoming interviews. The first of the interviews I was set to conduct was supposed to be with the Moroccan minister of social affairs, and had been scheduled for first thing on Monday morning. A rock formed in my chest as I imagined the bureaucratic nightmare that lay ahead if my suitcase wasn't found. I tried hard to remain hopeful and determined to get on with my work regardless. When morning finally came, I checked out of the hotel as it had posed yet another discomfort: an infestation of cockroaches in both the bathroom and the hotel reception area, these latter creatures taking the form of lusty men looking for prostitutes! This sight was not so unfamiliar in Morocco's touristic areas, but I had had enough of the disturbances at this point.

The next order of business involved calling London's Heathrow Airport to find out if my luggage had actually made it to Paris. A quick phone call confirmed that it had. I then called Orly Airport and after many attempts to get through, the answer finally came that since I had checked my luggage all the way to Rabat, then it must be that the suitcase had arrived in Morocco. It started to dawn on me that my suitcase had, most likely, been stolen at the airport in Rabat. By whom and how could I retrieve it? The answers to these questions I did not know.

To cut a long story short, I managed to borrow some recording equipment from the Arabic Service correspondent in Rabat, earlier in the morning of my scheduled interview with the minister. The equipment he was able to lend me were the older, much heavier type of recorders, producing a quality that was poor, to say the least. But I had no other choice and gratefully accepted them.

Nea'mat, the correspondent's sister-in-law, who had brought the equipment to me on his behalf, was a young and pleasant woman currently studying law. She was incredibly helpful throughout the entire ordeal as she used her Moroccan know-how to help me communicate with the officials in a way that she thought could make them cooperate better. You would think that my being Tunisian, a neighbouring country to Morocco, would come in handy but I came up against one brick wall after another in trying to track down my lost suitcase. Neighbourly compatriotism got me absolutely nowhere.

With the recording equipment arriving just in time, I managed to deliver the interview. At the end of the interview, I apologized to the minister for coming with the same clothes that I had travelled in two days before, as I felt they were too casual for the interview setting and probably still dishevelled from the long journey, in spite of my best efforts to freshen up the clothes. The minister, utterly shocked by this revelation, immediately asked her personal assistant to ring the airport and enquire about the suitcase. Nonetheless, her governmental influence yielded no results, as the answer from the airport remained the same: 'there is no suitcase!'

That afternoon after recording two more interviews, I accompanied Nea'mat to a nearby market to buy a change of clothes. The airlines could only offer me $50 as compensation for the lost luggage, which one official clarified was not meant to cover the value of the lost belongings, but to 'help me buy at least a toothbrush and toothpaste.'

For all of the five days that I was in Morocco travelling between various cities to interview people, I was still hoping that my luggage would be found in Morocco, or by some miracle returned to London after I had left. But that hope proved futile when I came back and some Moroccan friends told me that lost luggage was a regular occurrence, even for them as natives, and that they suspected that airport employees were the culprits of these common thefts. Usually they told me my friends did get at least some of their luggage back, but I was not so lucky.

Despite this hiccup, I feel particularly proud of the series of documentaries on people with special physical needs within the Arab world in 1999 – titled '*Disability: the power within*' as it was totally my own initiative — and was the first of its kind in the Arab world. It was re-broadcast several times by popular demand in various parts of the Arab world.

Why the interest in the topic? Since childhood, I have always taken a keen interest in issues concerning disabled people. I guess it was because I saw how they were treated either with disrespect and mockery or pity and marginalization. When I secured funding for the series and got the OK from my BBC Editor, I was really excited and committed myself to raise those issues the best way I could. More importantly, I was determined to highlight positive examples of people who managed to go beyond the restrictions imposed on them and the negative view they encountered to live life fully and be an example to others including those with no special needs. It was during this series that I met some of the most amazing and inspiring people. While on tour in Sudan, Lebanon and Morocco (the only three countries I got funding to visit), I met men and women with varying degrees and types of special needs. Two especially left a huge impact on me. They were both young women who became partially blind since childhood. However, they both managed to overcome that obstacle and lead normal and extremely independent lives.

Both Amani from Sudan and Nada from Lebanon had university degrees, interesting jobs and were very active in several organizations for people with special needs, each in her own country, the Arab world and Africa.

While Amani lived with her family, according to Arab tradition whereby a young woman only leaves her parents' house for her husband's, Nada lived on her own, did her cleaning, shopping as well as socializing. Nada also went on holidays with and without friends to so many fa-away places.

Amani who was less well-off, also travelled to many destinations in Africa and beyond as part of her work with NGOs (Non - governmental organizations). They were both single, but wanted to get married and start their own families. Both wanted as many as four children.

When I interviewed them, my first impression was how bubbly, positive and proactive they were. I talked and recorded them for hours without realizing how the time passed so quickly. I went away thinking that while some able-bodied people tend to forget that in every cloud, there's always a silver lining, here were these two women whose light was coming from within and it was what made them never lose hope. That was also the message that came across from the series.

Morocco in 1999

Impressions from the South of France

In 2001, I travelled to the South of France for a project that aimed to gauge French attitudes towards immigrants, particularly those of North African descent. These are some of the observations I recorded after my trip.

It had been the dream of every Tunisian girl growing up to go on holiday to La Cote D'Azur, the area of France incorporating Nice, Cannes and Monte Carlo. Their glamorous allure owed to the fact that they were known for being the hotspots of the rich and famous. I soon learned however that the general attitude of the French towards us as foreigners was less than glamourous. As I walked the streets of Nice, the unmistakable face of Zinedine Zidane, the French-Algerian footballer turned coach, was plastered everywhere advertising all kinds of products, from food to sports equipment. Zidane was a big star in France at the time ever since he scored the winning goals for France in the 1998 World Cup. Subsequently there had been a lot of noise in the media that the general French attitude towards foreigners especially North Africans would, as a result of this victory from a foreign-born French, change for the better. Such a turnaround in sentiment had been either slow in coming from what I saw, or simply not happening at all, at least in the South of France.

The North Africans who I met on this trip were even less enthused with the prospect of change. Some of them were born in France and had only vague memories of their parents' country of origin; the connection to the biological 'home' was barely apparent. Many North Africans told me that they were treated with suspicion by shopkeepers who followed them around the shops, checking if they were going to steal. These shopkeepers sometimes even snatched items from their hands and turned their backs to them when they came to pay, as a sign that they didn't want to serve them. As for routine harassment by the police, I witnessed that firsthand. In Nice, while waiting for a train to depart one afternoon, two armed French policemen boarded the train and began looking around menacingly. I thought there must be some kind of a dangerous criminal on the train by the hard expressions on their faces. Apparently, the suspected 'criminal' was a young man with distinctly North African looks who was sat by his wife and baby, waggling fingers at the small child who laughed, entertained. The two policemen walked straight towards him and urgently demanded to see his identity card. Very calmly, and without hesitation, he produced the card from a wallet in his coat. They snatched it from his hands and rained questions on him: where was he going, what was he going to do there and was he coming back? Apparently satisfied with his answers, they threw his identity card back at him and stormed off toward the next carriage.

Watching this scene, I felt blood rushing to my face and my entire body heating up. I was overcome with the urge to approach the two policemen and ask them what crime did the man commit to deserve this singling-out, but I also already knew that such a question was pointless, and would only result in drawing further unnecessary attention to the whole situation. Instead I stayed in my seat, dejected. I looked at the face of the accosted man, who was gazing into the air, smoking a cigarette. For a while, he did not talk to his wife or play with his baby, as he had been before the policemen had interrupted. The whole scene of familial bliss was marred by the sudden intrusion. The baby continued gurgling innocently, blissfully unaware of the level of humiliation that his father had just been subjected to. A new wave of helplessness washed over me as I thought of the colossal burden that this small baby had yet to inherit.

The calmness of this man in how he responded to racial profiling by the police was not new, nor was it isolated. Foreigners in France have come to expect this kind of treatment on a daily basis, but from what I gathered, they had definitely not accepted it. Among the North Africans that I met, there was a middle-aged Tunisian woman who had been living in France for over thirty years. She told me that she used to live in Paris and had decided to move to the South in the hope of being treated better in the sunnier part of France, only to be confronted with a new host of microaggressions and racial insults.

I also met a young Algerian woman named Samia, who had lived in Paris since the age of eight with her entire family. Samia was on holiday in Nice with her three-year-old daughter. Even though we only met briefly, the anger in her was like a hand grenade. We were about to get off the bus one day on our way to a nearby park, when the driver decided to close the doors and Samia, her daughter and I were trapped between them. She shouted to the driver to please wait. Instead of releasing the doors he hurled insults at us, calling us 'bloody foreigners' who should 'just go home!' in an angry stream of French. But he met his match in Samia who gave him an earful of verbal missiles. Though I was shocked at the driver's behaviour, I tried to calm Samia down, as she was physically shaking with rage. When we finally made it off the bus, the anger deflated out of Samia like a burst balloon, as she broke down into long-suppressed tears. She cried that she had had enough of this kind of treatment and asked if I could help her come and live in a better place like England.

At this request I was caught in a dilemma. The British police has been accused time and time again of racist policing and cultural insensitivity. An official report issued in 1999 after the killing of the Black British teenager, Stephen Lawrence on 22

April 1993, in a racially-motivated attack, linked the treatment of non-English Britons by police to institutionalized racism. The question of issuing residents of the United Kingdom who are over the age of eighteen with identity cards in 2002 provoked such uproar that the British government had to abandon the idea. It was seen by human rights groups as a violation of civil liberties. In France by comparison, having an identity card and carrying it all the time is absolutely essential especially if you happen to be of North African origin. I think that as immigrants we often develop a 'grass is greener' mentality about the various European capitals in which we find our diaspora, only to find that they are all quite similar in the problems we will inevitably encounter as foreigners.

Chapter 5

Answering a Call from a Rebel Leader

In June 2001, I joined the BBC African English department on secondment from my home department to produce two widely listened to live shows, *'Focus on Africa' and 'Network Africa'*. The editor of the programmes was a no-nonsense, inexplicably stern Englishman who almost everyone in the team feared because he never minced his harsh words. He was known for not taking calls from anyone with only two exceptions: people within positions of great influence, or his wife.

Soon into my secondment, I was working on *an edition of the news and current affairs programme 'Focus on Africa'* in the open plan office when the telephone rang. The voice on the other end was impressively strong, with deep, masculine timbres reverberating through the speaker. This captivating voice asked specifically to speak to the editor. When I asked for a name, he answered 'Dr Jonas Savimbi'. At the mention of his name I couldn't believe my ears. Taking a moment to collect myself and to make sure I got the name right, I repeated *'the* Dr Jonas Savimbi?!' 'Yes ma'am', he replied coolly in an accent that I couldn't quite work out. Immediately I called out to the editor who was sat in his small office, within the open plan office. He gruffly asked for a name without so much as turning around. 'Dr Jonas Savimbi.' I repeated yet again, waiting for his reaction but still in a state of dazzled disbelief. Upon hearing that, the editor jumped into action requesting that I put the call through at once.

The reason I was so overcome is because Dr Jonas Savimbi was the famed leader of UNITA, the National Union for the

Total Independence of Angola, the second-largest political party in the country. Founded in 1966, UNITA fought alongside the Popular Movement for the Liberation of Angola in the Angolan War for Independence and then again against the MPLA in the ensuing civil war. The war was one of the most prominent Cold War proxy wars, with UNITA receiving military aid from the United States and the white minority regime in South Africa before Nelson Mandela's release from prison, while the MPLA received support from the then Soviet Union and its allies. UNITA was headed by Dr Savimbi from its foundation, up until his death in 2002. Following Savimbi's death, UNITA abandoned the armed struggle and participated in electoral politics. Most recently, the party won seats in the 2008 parliamentary election.

Dr Savimbi had called the BBC African Service because he wanted the BBC to be the first to broadcast an important statement regarding the willingness of his movement to engage in talks with the government of Angola – the BBC considered one of the most trusted international media organizations. I was taken aback by his call because back in my home department, I was used to the frustrating process of chasing politicians, opposition figures and even just everyday commentators, without such efforts ever gaining fruition especially with politicians. I didn't interview Dr Savimbi myself, but on that day, from that phone call, I felt like a small part of something very powerful that can set agendas.

Chapter 6

Shifting Tides Back Home

Tunisians took to the streets in 2011 in what was the start of what became known as the 'Arab Spring'

I was still a member of staff at the BBC when the troubles in Tunisia started in late 2010-2011. I had just come back from a family holiday in the Canary Islands in mid-December when in no time, my usually quiet country of origin was being splashed all over the news channels as protests erupted in one city before rapidly advancing to the next, spreading like wildfire. The story behind the protests have been told seemingly over and over in the news, each outlet offering a slightly altered version from the other, but the following events are told exactly as I remember them.

The self- emulation of one young man on 17 December 2010 ignited mass protests all over the country. Mohammed Bouazizi – a street vendor- had burnt himself alive in protest at a system that had deprived him of a job to support himself, his mother, his stepfather and five siblings. This same system had also constantly humiliated him bureaucratically, by pestering him for a license for selling fruits and vegetables on the street. This has always been a requirement by the council of every city in the country.

The harrowing case of this 26-year-old resonated with many young unemployed men and women in Tunisia. It has become the norm that even the most accomplished university degree holders, who were previously the most employable of the country, graduated without any prospects for the future. Young people remain economically desolate while facing the enormous pressure of having their family relying on them for financial support. People from all walks of life took to the streets of most cities in the country, first demanding jobs, then the end of corruption and economic inequality, and finally the overthrow of the government which they felt had caused it all.

Most international media outlets like the BBC, Al-Jazeera, CNN, France 24 did not expect events in Tunisia to develop as dramatically and quickly as they did as the country hardly featured in the international news prior to that.

The only major demonstrations that the country had ever witnessed since its independence were when the Prime Minister under Bourguiba at the time, *Mohammed Mzali* decided to double the price of bread in 1984. Bread is essential to Tunisians and is the one food item that most Tunisians cannot do without. Hardly a meal goes without bread.

Thousands rioted, riot police fired at protesters, but people did not back down and within days, the government was forced to go back to the original price.

The riots of December 2010- early January 2011 on the other hand, were much bigger and far more significant from what I saw. I watched while protesters threw stones at the security forces, the latter retaliating with live ammunition. The sheer amount of force used by the security men in heavy and dark gear never seen before this, was extremely unsettling. One particular picture haunted me: some protesters fleeing while members of the security forces in civilian clothes were chasing them. A young man fell to the ground and was brutally attacked by those in pursuit.

For days and nights, I was glued to the television screen watching developments unfold, while constantly calling my family back home to check that they were all safe. Suddenly London felt one million miles away from home and it was especially agonising to watch the news while feeling utterly powerless to all of the devastation happening back home.

On Friday 14 January, I watched while history was made when it was reported that President Ben Ali had stepped down and was leaving the country. The military maintained an omnipresence in Tunisia's towns and cities. A video of a prominent lawyer walking up and down the empty main avenue in Tunis, Avenue Habib Bourguiba, late that night, shouting 'Ben Ali fled' sent shivers down my spine. Avenue Habib Bourguiba is usually flooded with people spilling out of its shops and cafes, and the road is always rammed with traffic lodged in its lanes. But in that moment not a single soul walked its tree-lined street as the man chanted Tunisia's new reality over and over. The video was broadcast by several international media outlets, moved people both in Tunisia and abroad, to tears and later became a symbol of what's referred as Tunisia's 'revolution'.

I will never forget how the national TV station on that same night changed its name from Tunisia7 – named after the date

Ben Ali came to power on 7 November 1987 – to the Tunisian National Television. And the change did not just include the name — some faces that were known to be close to Ben Ali's government, who had over the years, become almost synonymous with the channel suddenly disappeared, replaced by new faces we had never seen before. On that same night, the station hosted a live debate that questioned everything and everyone – something unheard of under Ben Ali- including one of its main presenters. He was put on the spot about his role in being Ben Ali's defender on the channel. This style of programming came across as retribution.

Watching that for the first time, with the fundamental changes in the media scene that soon followed, it felt like a true revolution was actually unfolding in my country of origin.

The dramatic events in Egypt that took place soon after in January 2011 and then Libya in February of the same year in what became known as 'The Arab Spring', left many Tunisians feeling that the strong winds of change came from Mohammed Bouazizi's city Sidi Bouzid, located in central Tunisia.

Just as I vividly remember those events, I also remember the day Ben Ali became President in a bloodless coup on 7 November 1987. I was on a night shift the night before and had been sleeping for most of the following day as a result. As soon as I awoke, I put the radio on as I always have done. On *BBC Arabic*, it was a major headline and they called it a 'white' coup. The colour white meant that it wasn't violent and the reason given for the coup was that Bourguiba was unfit to rule for health reasons. I remember feeling very concerned and thinking that this wasn't good news because Ben Ali had a military background, and he wasn't nearly as charismatic or educated as Bourguiba. How would he maintain the same level of efficiency without Bourguiba's innate political adeptness? I called my family that evening to make sure they were all safe.

As I recall, mixed feelings about the change of leader were common and widespread.

Why am I citing these events here, you may wonder? Because throughout my career at the BBC, my home country rarely featured in the news, I guess because it was uniquely trouble-free in an ever-troubled region. In fact, I always asked consecutive British heads of the BBC Arabic Service about the reason behind broadcasting to the country and to the entire Maghreb on short wave, which was static and declining in the face of modern technology.

So, to see my country of origin making the headlines of not just BBC Arabic, but all the other language services including the *World Service in English, Al-Jazeera English, CNN, France 24 and* every single media outlet in the world when just before that, many people globally didn't even know where Tunisia was on the world map, left me with mixed feelings. Suddenly, journalists from other departments within the BBC started calling the Arabic Service looking for Tunisian journalists to give background information. There were still very few of us at the time and we all suddenly became 'experts' on Tunisian affairs.

I was glad about the political change and proud because it came as a result of a popular movement, but I also had misgivings about what was coming because I didn't think that there existed a better alternative. People just wanted to get rid of the 'dictator'. I felt that the change was based more on emotions because people had had enough of Ben Ali and his family. The fact that many Tunisians are now nostalgic about Ben Ali's era, as I find every time I go back to visit or talk to family and friends, just goes to prove that.

At the time, I only wished that my home country had made the news headlines for something more promising: more stability, prosperity and widespread socio-economic development.

Chapter 7

San Diego

Since leaving the BBC in 2011, I have been working as a freelance journalist for various places. One of them is the Africa Leadership Centre at Kings College, London.

In October 2015, the Centre sent me to San Diego, California to cover a conference on the study of Africa and whether those studies reflected the changes the continent was witnessing. It was my first trip to the USA, and San Diego was nothing like any place I had visited before. Everything felt supersized, it was like being in wonderland: the roads, the cars, the stores, everything was huge. Villas with sprawlingly immaculate front lawns lined the avenues and what appeared to be normal convenience stores from the exterior, sold everything inside from touristy t-shirts to rifle guns. The streets were almost deserted except for a scattering of American tourists, and the weather was particularly warm, in spite of the autumn season.

To my pleasant surprise I discovered that this particular city was only a twenty-minute drive away from the closest Mexican town. I was tempted to visit as I rarely ever found myself in this corner of the world. I was warned by locals though that the town in question, Tijuana, was really rough. When a fellow participant at the conference noticed my keen interest, he asked why I would want to be in a place full of crime when I could just wander around the very safe, comparably posh San Diego instead. So-called 'posh' areas are generally of little interest to me as an investigative journalist!

The conference ended on Sunday morning and most of the participants started to make the journey home that same day. My flight back to London was not until the evening of the following day. After breakfast, I packed my things, checked out of the room and left my suitcase at reception. Still deliberating, I requested a taxi and when the driver arrived, I found out from him that San Diego was home to the biggest aquarium in the world, which could round off my trip. So, I thought of seeking his opinion: whether to play it safe and go to the aquarium or be adventurous and go to the Mexican border. The driver, an Ethiopian immigrant to San Diego, said he could take me to the latter, but warned that I should leave Mexico before three o'clock that afternoon. He explained that it might be difficult to re-enter the American border after that time due to the long queues of Mexicans looking for work, of whom most are denied entry. I thanked him and tried not to forget that valuable piece of information. In the car, I was both excited at the prospect of spontaneously visiting yet another new place.

On the way there, the driver told me that San Diego was filled with other African immigrants. Apparently, the shared warm climate between California and most of Africa made Africans from the Horn and sub-Saharan African countries mostly looking for work, feel that this part of the USA was like home.

After a short while, a simple border crossing formed on the horizon. At this long-anticipated border stood only a cabin with an officer inside and no signpost, or indication of any kind, to show that I crossed into a totally different country. Just as easy as it had been in Kuwait all those years ago in 1994, I had arrived at the Mexican border without any great fanfare, and yet the excitement that rippled through me was palpable.

Although I have been fortunate enough to see much of the world through my work, the excitement I feel in new places reminds me of the young girl who grew up always dreaming of faraway places, all so large and grandiose compared to Tunisia's tiny occupation on the map.

As soon as I got my passport back from the officer in the tiny cabin, I considered the most time-efficient way to see as much as possible in the meagre three hours or so I had before I had to get back. I soon stopped a taxi and asked him to take me on a tour of Tijuana. It was my own good luck that the first taxi I could flag had a driver who spoke English; my Spanish by comparison was too patchy for me to rely on. As we drove on, I emphasized the need to be back before three o'clock, to which the driver reassured me that we would be.

Some parts of the city were rough indeed: prostitutes operating openly in broad day light, rundown houses, piles of litter strewn in the streets. The driver also took me to the Mexican side of the Pacific. The water was pristine, but I was shocked to see that the notorious concrete wall was built running along the border and right through the ocean, dividing Mexico from the USA. Coast guards on the American side were carefully watching from small windows overlooking the two sides of the ocean, guns swinging in their arms. From my vantage point outside the taxi, I saw a young Mexican couple walking hand in hand on the beautiful beach, being carried away. As soon as they came within metres of the wall, a guard alarmingly shouted to them to immediately move back! The contradictions in this scene filled me with sadness.

There were no major landmarks to see as it was a very poor city at my time of visiting, but just as taxi drivers anywhere in the world think and behave, this medium height, dark-haired, middle-aged man kept suggesting new places to visit that he insisted were worthwhile. The last place he took me to looked like a big factory, producing what? I didn't know, and he didn't say.

At this point, I insisted to be taken back. He finally obliged, speeding through the wide streets to make it back in time. When I got to the crossing point at around a quarter to three, the queues were already very long. One tall American man in the already densely packed queue explained to me that there were three different queues: one for US and European citizens, one for Mexicans and the third for disabled people and those with mobility issues. On the Mexican side of the crossing, the security guards had dogs sniffing at every Mexican in the queue. I found it de-humanizing that only the Mexican queue should face this treatment, casting my mind back to the only North African man on the train in Nice, in 2001.

With my British passport, I joined the first of the queues but one glance ahead at the sheer number of people, I simply wondered if I was going to make it. Precisely at that point, a Mexican man caught my attention as he was walking along the queues asking if anyone wanted to make it to the top of the queue for only $6. I was ready to jump at the opportunity but was sceptical of its legitimacy, to which the man pointed to an 8-seater white Toyota, already half-full of passengers. I felt reassured when I saw another woman smiling in the front seat. I paid the $6, left the queue and took my seat inside the car. We waited for a few minutes for the car to fill up further. In no time however, we were on our way. Rejoining the long queue at its front, but thankfully it went by quickly and before I knew it, I was on the other side.

I was utterly relieved to be out of the crossing and ran to flag the first taxi I found. The driver was half Afghan and half Iranian and had immigrated to the USA decades before. He would have easily passed for a Mexican if not for his substantial height. He said he suffered racism all the time where he was stopped and questioned by the police while out driving. He attributed this treatment to his looks and also his name. As the end of the journey neared, he asked me what I was in Mexico for. When I told him, he repeated the same qualms that I had heard from my colleague about Tijuana being dangerous, but I felt no regrets about going there. No amount of warnings could have quelled my journalistic impulses anyway, regardless of my trepidation! Thankfully I made it to the airport with time to spare, and a story to tell.

Years later I narrated this experience to a friend who remarked that he never travelled to a place where he didn't know anyone. I replied that if I did that, I would never have even left Tunis!

San Diego 2015 , The Wall that separates the USA from Mexico

Chapter 8

Love and Marriage

London is not only the place where I started my career, but is also the city in which I met my late husband, the well-known Pan-Africanist, the charismatic Dr Tajudeen Abdul-Raheem. We met for the first time at the British Labour Party Conference in October 1989. Based in the coastal city of Brighton, the yearly conference was my first ever reporting trip for BBC Arabic. Tajudeen on the other hand was reporting on behalf of one of the many African magazines he was freelancing for at the time. In a strange set of coincidences, I was accompanied by an older, male, Jordanian colleague, and Tajudeen also happened to be in the presence of an older lady throughout the conference, who I had initially presumed to be his partner.

Tajudeen and I on the London tube in the early 1990s

Arab and North African customs traditionally dictate that out of respect for my colleague, in spite of us sharing an entirely professional and platonic relationship, talking to Tajudeen in my colleague's presence would have been disrespectful. So, although Tajudeen's unmistakable gap-toothed smile caught my attention, I travelled home after the conference resigned to the thought that I would probably never see him again.

About two weeks later I was sat on the Piccadilly Line during my morning commute, in my betrothed seat: the one closest to the doors in the second carriage from the front, same as always. My mind was by now long purged of any thoughts of the charismatic stranger from the conference, as the nonstop activity of daily life always ensures. Thumbing through Dostoyevsky's classic, *The Brothers Karamazov,* I noticed that a person sitting in the opposite row was trying to catch my attention.

Anyone who is familiar with the London tube will understand the classic Londoner hostility on public transport which I had picked up in a matter of months, so I was wary of this waving stranger. To my complete surprise, I looked up to find Tajudeen smiling at me as if we were lifelong friends. The impossibility of the situation preceded me — I mean, of all places to bump into a totally unfamiliar face from Brighton, in my designated spot on my daily commute, no less! He smiled at me, revealing that memorable gap in his shining white teeth. Too shy to return the smile, I buried my face in my book, feeling my face beginning to burn. Tajudeen was seated with a friend of his who, I later learned, was visiting from Nigeria. As the two got up to leave, Tajudeen waved to me again and in a rolling gesture with his index fingers, indicated that we would meet again. I remember being taken aback by his complete unabashed forwardness, a trait so polar opposite to my innate tentativeness.

Life proceeded as normal until one blisteringly cold Friday evening in November 1989. I had gone to the Africa Centre – based in Covent Garden at the time- for a panel discussion after finishing a day shift. The Centre hosted debates, art exhibitions, live music concerts and had a bar and a restaurant in the basement. It was only a short walk from where the BBC World Service was based in Bush House, on the Strand. As I approached the famous brown building, I was stunned by the unfamiliar sight of Tajudeen once again, standing outside the wide doors with a friend of his. At this point I was starting to feel overwhelmed by all of the coincidences; that fate should put this random man in my path three times now in different places was perplexing to my rational, straightforward mind. Still extremely puzzled, I turned around to head back to the station, foregoing the panel discussion altogether.

As I was heading in the opposite direction, Tajudeen ran to catch up with me. 'Excuse me but, I think I know you,' came the commanding timbre of his voice. 'No, you don't' I replied. 'Can I interest you in our *Revolutionary Banner* for only 20 pence?', he pressed. In his hand was a small white booklet with red writing on it, and among the words on its cover the word '*Socialism*' stood out to me. I politely declined not because I didn't like socialism, in fact the opposite is true, but to avoid what felt like a strange set of coincidences and kept walking.

The *Revolutionary Banner* was produced by the United Revolutionary Front of Ghana and the Editor was his very good friend from Ghana, *Napoleon Abdulai* who was standing there. He gave me one of his infectious smiles, picking up his pace to keep up. 'You can have it for free and maybe you would want to attend this interesting panel discussion that is about to start? It could be useful for your work since you are a journalist, like me'.

Tajudeen, the orator and Pan-Africanist

He seemed to remember this common detail from the conference. I did not tell him then that that's what I was there for, but thought to myself maybe I could go in and listen for a short period of time then leave. Abandoning the discussion all together on account of my initial apprehension would be futile as the material could be useful for one of my weekly programmes anyway.

Tajudeen had also put me at some degree of ease as he was so accustomed to doing. All this time, *Napoleon* was standing close by, with his hands folded behind his back, watching expressionless. Tajudeen introduced us and I found out that, together with a group of other African men and women, they were a group of young activists working on addressing issues of military rule, corruption, inequality, gender issues amongst a wealth of other issues within their home countries and the continent at large. As they say, the rest is history!

Mine and Tajudeen's union brought up a spectrum of different reactions from people. It was extremely rare in my home country for a Tunisian girl to marry a man from sub-Saharan Africa. Anti-blackness is rife in the Arab World and so there was confusion about our relationship. The fact that Nigeria is an Anglophone country invited even more questions; if I had to marry outside of Tunisia, wouldn't it be easier to choose someone with a similarly Francophone heritage? The two sides perceived each other as if they had nothing in common whatsoever.

According to a *'World Atlas'* article published in 2018, The phrase "North African Arabs" describes people who live in the Maghreb region in North Africa and speak a dialect of Arabic as their native language. These people identify as Arabs. This identity can be attributed to the Arabs conquering and occupying North Africa and the subsequent spread of Islam in Africa. Arab tribes migrated to Africa in the 11th century in the Maghreb region such as Bani Hilal, Beni Hassan, and Bani Sulaym.

The Maghreb region of Africa refers to Northwest Africa, and is composed of Mauritania, Morocco, Algeria, Tunisia, and Libya. The region is often referred to as the *"Greater Maghreb"* in Arabic. It has a population of over 100 million people as of 2017.

Despite this large number of Arabs living in Africa, most of them do not identify themselves as Africans and many Africans do not see them as such either. People in North Africa generally consider themselves to be Arabs, Mediterranean or Amazigh, or all of those identities and more all mixed together. People of sub-Saharan Africa by comparison regard North Africans as non-Africans and point out to the oppression and discrimination against black Africans across the Maghreb especially in Mauritania and Libya.

In spite of the frontline role played by the late Libyan leader, Colonel Gaddafi, in bringing about the Union of African States, sentiments against Africans (particularly West African immigrants) have always exposed the vast chasm between popular feelings and the official position. These sentiments continued after the collapse of Gaddafi's rule in 2011 and for years later as thousands of Sub-Saharan African immigrants and workers have found themselves trapped in Libya as the fighting between opposing parties escalated.

In spite of its rarity, there have been instances of Tunisian girls marrying men from Francophone Africa, such as Senegal, Côte D'Ivoire, and so on. Having French as a common language between the two can encourage a relationship, but even these seemingly more 'natural' relationships were widely uncommon at my time of meeting Tajudeen. Thus, it was simply unheard of for a Tunisian girl to marry a Nigerian man. If it were vice versa, and a Tunisian man were to marry a Nigerian girl, perhaps it would have been more palatable to our audience of immediate family, relatives and neighbours back home. This is due to the elevated status of boys in the family and the right it gives them to go against the grain in a way that is unacceptable, and ultimately dishonourable, for girls and women.

In Sefsari, the traditional Tunisian dress preparing for the wedding ceremony

As a result of all of these external factors, mine and Tajudeen's relationship was met with friction. Looking back, I think my mother in particular was concerned about what the rest of the extended family would think and say — the honour of the family was resting on how this decision was received, after all. The general misconception of Black African men back home was that they were polygamous, so my mother assumed that Tajudeen was already married to at least one woman in his home country. Compounded by this was the impression that since I had moved to Europe, though not very common and still frowned upon, it would not have come as a huge surprise if I brought home a white man. All he needed to do was to convert to Islam. Our decision to be together just made no sense to my family back home.

After a lot of figurative pushing and shoving, I did finally manage to convince them that he was a good man, and he proved that to them himself. He was extremely respectful towards my late parents in spite of all the presumptions. He was always very jovial and brought a happy energy to my family home during his first visit to Tunisia. After a couple of meetings, his upbeat energy and relentless humour prevailed through the language barriers and preconceived notions that separated him from my family, and my parents and siblings alike found him exceptional and a larger than life personality. The fact that he was a fellow Muslim and always greeted my parents in the Muslim way (*Assalamu Alaykum*), also left an impression on them.

Our wedding ceremony in Tunis in August 1994 was an international affair. Apart from members of my family and friends, the guest list included some of Tajudeen's siblings, who travelled from Nigeria in a long-winded flight via Europe, his friends and work colleagues from Nigeria, Ghana, Zanzibar and the United Kingdom.

Our wedding ceremony in Tunis 1994

Our wedding – an international affair

I travelled home first to prepare for the wedding ceremony. T*ajudeen* known for doing everything 'lastminute.com' – everyone knew this about him, but I did not expect him to be late for his own wedding too! He was on an official mission in Uganda and returned to London before catching a flight to Tunisia on the same day.

I was very worried when everyone arrived at the hotel where we held the wedding reception except him. When he eventually showed up in his loose white Nigerian attire and matching cap-made from the same material and with the same design – and sat next to me, I asked him what caused the delay and told him of my embarrassment. "'Where is the problem, my friend?'" (he used to call me that and I used to protest that I was his fiancée /wife not his friend) he answered, "'My brother could have happily stepped in and no one would have noticed'", he continued in his usual humour.

The resemblance between Tajudeen and his younger brother, the late Sikiru Abdul-Raheem in the features, the voice and the mannerism, was indeed striking!

When Alejandra, my best friend from Uruguay arrived at Carthage airport in Tunis, she had to show the officers - who had never met anyone from that part of the world and only heard of it through the football World Cup tournaments- a tiny dot on her passport where her country was on the world map. As for my family – immediate and extended- they were simply fascinated by the mix of nationalities present.

I travelled to his *Tajudeen's* hometown, *Funtua*, located in *Katsina* State in northern Nigeria for the first time in September of 1995, unaccompanied by Tajudeen. He had been banned from visiting the country due to a series of highly incendiary criticisms of military rule in Nigeria especially the annulment of the results of democratic elections on June 12 1993, by the then military ruler. Severely criticizing military rule in Africa and anywhere in the world and their non -democratic practices was something Tajudeen did without fear.

Confronted with a similar language barrier, his Yoruba and Hausa-speaking parents and I had difficulty communicating, but I sensed genuine warmth from them from the very beginning. His parents were Yoruba by origin, who had migrated to the North where Hausa is spoken predominantly. I found it easier to pick up words and phrases in Hausa than Yoruba due to the former's similarity to Arabic in its vocabulary, although the pronunciation is different.

I stayed with various members of Tajudeen's family spread out between Kano, Zaria, Kaduna, Ibadan, Abuja and Lagos, summoning stares from people on the street wherever I went. Kids in particular were very curious about me and followed me in every house I stayed in, calling me *baturiya* before erupting into giggles, a Hausa term for 'white/European woman.' When I found out the meaning of the word, I protested that I was Tunisian, and brown for that matter! Tajudeen's family laughed these protests off as they explained that anyone who wasn't black, was seen as white. There was no in between. The novelty of seeing a fair-skinned person is something I still encounter when I have gone to visit in more recent years.

The complications with my name persisted even in Nigeria. If my name in the UK typically became Maureen or Monica, Moira or Marina, in Nigeria I was crowned Munirat, Muniratu or Maimouna! The last being the closest to my heart. It was a much closer variation at least.

****

Years later Tajudeen and I had two daughters, Aida and Ayesha. When Aida was little and started going to nursery, she couldn't understand why her Afro hair, as a result of her being mixed-race, was different to that of her English friends. One winter day while driving her home from nursery, Aida made an announcement from the backseat. 'Mum, I want to have hair like Chloe's.' Chloe was a girl in Aida's nursery, with very straight, almost white-blonde hair. I wasn't expecting the declaration at all; I figured that identity questions would come along a bit later on in the girls' childhood or teen years. I asked her why. 'Because Chloe has beautiful straight blond hair.' Aida responded, resolute. 'Chloe has blonde straight hair, and you have dark curly hair, and you're *both* beautiful.' I reminded her, eyeing her in the rearview mirror to check that she had understood.

Back home in Tunis for our summer holidays: My late mother and brother Miled,
Tajudeen, Aida and Ayesha

Obviously, the girls looked different to many of their peers; being mixed-race was no longer as rare as it had been, but the new norm was Black and white mixed-race, as opposed to Black and North African.

70

After ruminating on my words, Aida asked 'why is my hair different from hers?' Cautious not to make my daughter feel any different from anyone else, and in order to prevent the onset of an identity crisis from an early age, I paused before replying 'because God made us all very different and if we all looked the same, the world would be a very boring place.' To which Aida exclaimed 'but God is not a hairdresser!' She had me there. I couldn't find a satisfactory answer to her rightful claim, but kept laughing all the way home.

Aida having her hair platted while Ayesha watches

More importantly, I hoped that Aida and her younger sister Ayesha would not have an issue with their hair and skin colour when they grow up or feel they don't fit in their schools, friendship circles or the society as a whole. They did go through a period when they felt the need to straighten their hair or have an extension, but it was more for practical reasons especially during revision and exam time. Now though, they are happy with their natural hair and wear it with pride.

An early family photo in London with Aida

Chapter 9

Identity

After having spent the majority of my life in the UK, I'm constantly asked whether I feel more Tunisian or more British, and I am often asked to choose between the two.

Before and during Brexit, a number of surveys were conducted on the British character, whether the British felt European and why many voted to leave the European Union. One of them by *ProjectBritain.com*.

The British are said to be reserved in manners, dress and speech. They are famous for their politeness, self-discipline and especially for their humour. British people have a strong sense of humour which sometimes can be hard for foreigners to understand.[1]

The British are also known globally as a reserved, traditional and conventional people, all characteristics that culminate in extreme patience.

From my own observations, British people queue for everything, whatever the weather even if the queue is a kilometre long. Also, from my own impressions, the British can be guided by organization and sticking to the rules in almost everything they do, especially when it comes to safety and security and it's all very important.

According to a questionnaire conducted by the British Council in recent years, British people are most recognized for *'their good manners, dry sense of humour, love of alcohol, pride in their country and unappetizing cuisine.'* Alternatively, they are considered

---

[1] http://projectbritain.com/index/people.htm#gsc.tab=0

to be *'friendly, well-educated and law-abiding,'* according to the same questionnaire.

The English language is also largely noncommittal, containing a lot of neutral expressions. One example that I keep encountering usually occurs when a person changes their appearance. Remarking about someone's new haircut, people here tend to say, *'you look rather different.'* From those two words: *'rather'* and *'different'*, in my early years of living here, I could not work out whether this feedback is positive or negative. The same is true of the expression *'that's rather interesting'*, another frequent saying. I always ask if that means good or bad, as people rarely elaborate on in what way it is *interesting*.

To the average Brit, privacy and personal space is of utmost importance. Speaking from my own experience, you can live next to a British person for decades and it would be completely normal to not know what the inside of their home looks like. Years could pass without you knowing what they really think about anything, or even about you for that matter. Politeness can often function as a barrier to conversations about sensitive or personal topics, which can make it more difficult to establish a deeper connection. I think this is why a conversation between strangers usually starts with the weather. Yes, British weather is famously unpredictable, but talking about the weather is a classically British way of avoiding talking about personal matters and remaining on neutral ground.

Tunisians by comparison are immediately friendly, approachable and open. They will often talk to you as if they have known you all their lives even when you are meeting for the first time! Some Tunisians can feel comfortable enough to ask you quite personal questions from the first meeting by way of friendliness in some situations, or by way of nosiness in others. Politeness manifests totally differently for Tunisians than it does Brits, where the former will often invite you into their family home to meet several of their relatives, even if they don't know you well. Tunisians generally have little respect for personal space especially on public transport; orderly queues generally do not exist.

I always say that Tunisians operate too much outside the box, where the average Tunisian would always look for an alternative way to do things, and anyone who has been on Tunisian roads would understand what I mean, while the Brits too much inside it. The struggle of my dual identity tries to meet somewhere in the middle.

So, to the age-old identity question, I simply reply that I am both: a British Tunisian, or a Tunisian Brit, whichever way you want to package it. When I'm in Tunisia, the Tunisian in me immediately resurfaces: I respond to people's friendliness without any barriers, and banter back and forth in the classically sarcastic Tunisian sense of humour. I enthusiastically haggle in the *souq* and go to the *hammam* and enjoy the experience as fully as if I had never left.

To Tunisians, it's always strikingly obvious that I live elsewhere because of the way I behave in public: I queue, I give priority on the road and in public places, speak in a low volume and give notice to my siblings and relatives before I visit, rather than showing up at their doorstep without prior warning or announcement. I don't get worked up as quickly or easily anymore, like the infamous hot temper that our people share, and try not to take things personally.

I also tend to be more challenging of long-held beliefs, traditions and behaviours which can be irksome to friends and family back home, as many haven't had exposure to other cultures.

In the UK, I am both aware and proud of my origins as I feel that I carry my heritage with me wherever I go in my name, my appearance, my hybridised accent and manner of speaking.

I don't mind these signifiers at all and never sought to change them because I see them as expressions of my own individuality.

I have also been asked the age - old question often asked of bi- and tri-linguals: whether I think in Arabic or English. Well, French has taken a back seat since I came to work and live in London over three decades ago and only comes back to life when I am in France or in a French-speaking country. I can say I have a good command of the English language, however there are certain situations where I feel I can only express myself properly in Tunisian Arabic: when I am very excited or very angry and as in the case of most bilingual people living outside their countries: counting! Such is the nature of a dual identity.

With international friends at a Tunisian restaurant in London before lockdown

Epilogue

It has been quite a journey both professionally and personally. But what it has taught me is beyond what words can describe. I am grateful, happy and proud to have done it and to have followed my dream. Had I not followed my heart, only God knows how my life would be today.

In my personal life, I have always been eager to learn and try new things and new approaches and meet new people from cultures that are very different to mine. Because of that, I have grown so much and still growing for I believe as long as one lives, the learning never stops.

As a journalist, working widely for the BBC and numerous other outlets equally, I have always applied principles of objectivity, accuracy, credibility, fairness, neutrality and balance in every program and news bulletin I have worked on, interview I have conducted or given and article I have written. Now as a freelancer, I train new journalists on those principals and how these help us tell stories with authority. Above all, my mission remains the same as when I first started: to always ingrain real passion for the profession.

Throughout my career, I have relentlessly been endeavouring to raise awareness, seeking to make people question their preconceived ideas and taboos, and seizing every opportunity to challenge policymakers about the need for reform and positive change. Over the years, many of these efforts have garnered responses, namely that of the King of Morocco, Mohammed VI when he introduced new laws in 1999 to give disabled people in his country a quota of jobs in the public sector after the documentaries I produced on the issue in Morocco was broadcast.

I have always enjoyed being in the field talking to real people about real issues; amplifying the voices of those who have been rendered voiceless especially in the Arab world, who represent a large section of their societies, and yet have little visibility. Turning this conviction into groundbreaking programs has always driven me more than anything.

That, for me, is what journalism is truly all about. Have I stopped or will I ever stop being a journalist? Never!

Praise for this Book

An exciting narrative of an experienced journalist which takes the reader through different cultures and civilizations – her upbringing in her native country of Tunisia and acculturation to the British society where she has lived and worked as a journalist and reporter for the influential BBC for many years.

Her account of how she met and married the highly progressive and articulate pan-Africanist, the late Dr. Tajudeen Abdul-Raheem, with whom they had two daughters-Aida and Ayesha-cannot but get the reader wondering if certain events were, indeed, decided by forces beyond human control.

In this fluent and concise book of diverse issues of society and identities, Mounira Chaieb has deployed the expertise of the competent journalist that she is to entertain and enrich our knowledge of the wonderful world we live in.

I have profited immensely from reading this book and believe others undoubtedly will too.

Anthony A. Akinola, Author of several books on political issues
Oxford, UK

NO! not every taxi driver in London is called Roger! Nor every Tunisian blurb up such a beautiful literary work in a foreign tongue either.

What an eloquent non-fiction piece of work, this is!

Mounira Chaieb has reduced life-long experiences of a female Maghrebi immigrant in the hustle and bustle of London- which stereotypically speaking should have been daunting even for a male migrant- to something that's not only cheerful, albeit peppered with some serious moments, but a delightful read also.

I have known Mounira Chaieb for a number of years through the BBC and also as a friend. I knew she is a bubbly personality, but this book has opened a new window for me onto her humour, which was not apparent, before reading these gripping pages.

Considering the many hiccups life has thrown at her, not least the loss of her husband in a horrific way, leaving her with their two girls at a tender age, I would have expected the narration of this book to be melancholic at best. The inner self of the writer seems to defy reality and aid her plume to, instead, draw something witty.

It is to be unquestionably admired, that someone could elaborate and juggle so agilely, between situations and moments, sometimes mundane and sometimes thought-provoking, as Chaieb has done while writing the chapters of this book when you realise that English is not her first language, nor her second, but her third after Arabic and French. A few could go into the detail of things, as wittingly, as she has done in this semi- autobiography (with a twist), without tumbling over language barriers.

Until I read these pages, I thought I knew enough about Mounira Chaieb's ups and downs, both in the UK, where we met and worked together and later became friends, and in Tunisia, where she was born and grew up. However, she succeeded, in an impressive way, to grab my attention and take me along with her many journeys, tribulations and joys and wanting to know more.

Conveying the ins and outs of what the 'Jasmine' Revolution meant for her touched my heart, as it would do to the hearts of all advocates for people's freedoms and rights. But reducing my appreciation of this book to just this one angle is not fair on the other episodes of the book. I wonder if it's greed, or the accounts are that compelling, that I sometimes wanted to learn more about certain settings in the manuscript. Or could it be a subtle scheme Mounira Chaieb eschewed to let the readers want more?

In any case, I shall read the book and read it and read it again and recommend it to all those who leave their country and childhood home for a better life abroad or those who want to know that foreigners and migrants can – like Mounira Chaieb – contribute to their economy and library as well.

Rachid Sekkai, Senior BBC Arabic Journalist

Mounira has the gift of writing in a way that transports us straight into her narrative, so that we experience it as if we were there.

Kate Pemberton, Director, Collage Writing Room. London

How beautifully Mounira captures the essence of every event, thought and emotion... I was immediately transported on her journey.

Mounira writes so exquisitely, she is a true word-smith. Everything that she has written and shared with me, I could feel every word and nuance and have immediately been transported on her journey. I feel so proud to know Mounira, she's a truly a creative, imaginative and gifted woman. Beautiful writing, well done.

Ms Koula Refahi, Mentor and friend. London

The book is an excellent account of the synthesis of identity, from the complex social structure of Tunis to the alien structures of the UK, from a largely traditional Muslim society to a dominantly free UK.

Mounira's marriage to the Nigerian Pan-Africanist, Tajudeen Abdul-Raheem, added to the complexity, but resulted in a successful synthesis, due to the enhanced social consciousness of an empowered woman.

The book is highly recommended.

Patrick Wilmot, writer and commentator on Pan – African and political affairs

Prior to having the privilege of reading the semi-autobiography "with a difference" of my friend Mounira Chaieb, I thought that, after 33 years of friendship, I knew her reasonably well. "No, you don't," I can hear her say, as she had said to her husband to be in the early days of their relationship.

Going through the labyrinths of her amazing journey from the streets of Cité Ezzouhour in Tunis, when she was a young girl witnessing sexist practices and rubbing shoulders with marginalised groups, such as women, the disabled, and the down-trodden, she was "silently" wishing to have the power one day to address these issues.

Before becoming a powerful radio voice, radio came to her home in Tunis when she was a child and represented one of her two windows to learn about the world, and later contribute as much as possible to highlight, raise awareness, and change some of its unjust practices. The second window was her love for languages as a means to broaden her horizons through building bridges with other people and cultures through communication.

From dreams through story-telling, radio and "devouring" world literature, Mounira Chaieb landed a job with the London-based BBC Arabic Service, followed a few years later with a secondment to Focus on Africa among other departments, which brought her from the periphery to centre stage, where her curiosity, linguistic expertise and fascination with radio, were going to be put to good use.

Realizing the great potential and impact of her job, Mounira Chaieb very quickly made a clear choice for documentaries and investigative journalism where she could see much scope for creativity and impact, through getting out, meeting real people and dealing with real issues. Her longing to move on to the world stage, brought continents, countries, world cities, people and cultures much closer, as she was able to travel to remote places in North Africa, Sub - Saharan Africa, the Middle East, Europe and even the Americas.

True to herself, Mounira focused on issues of injustice, taboos, honour killings, female circumcision, disability, drug abuse, sex education and much more. In her search for diverse views and perspectives on these issues, she sought the views of all kinds of people ranging from heads of state, ministers, senior politicians, opposition figures, UNHCR, artists, writers, sportspeople, and lay men and women.

Mounira Chaieb's narration goes from the personal to the general, and vice versa. She moves in a pleasant, gentle, and seamless way from one issue to the other, and from one region to the other without shocking or disturbing the reader.

She is very good at letting the story of the moment shed more light on her interested, compassionate, and caring personality. Among other interesting and touching stories, I was very much impressed by the two ladies in her series: Disability – the Power Within. Read the book to find out more.

Mounira Chaieb can also pick up the funny side of some of her experiences by generously sharing them with the reader in succinct and funny ways. Her explanation of the title of her book "Is Every Cab Driver Called Roger," is one of them, which I found hilarious. The warning she received in Cairo about the risk of being eaten by crocodiles in Sudan, her experience with the Limousine in Stockholm, her realisation about Shakespeare's English and Cockney in London, and others never fail to put a smile on the reader's face.

Mounira Chaieb also experienced difficult times through this journey, not least her choice to go and have a career in London, and her decision to tie the knot with a Nigerian activist, which both worried and saddened her mum, at an initial stage, at least. Her experience in the streets of the Kuwaiti capital, the loss of a suitcase during her travel to Morocco and how she resolved the problem, and her decision to visit a "rough" Mexican town despite the advice given to her by a number of people, are all proof of a brave lady who once replied to a friend who told her that he never goes to places where he does not know anyone that "if I did that, I would never have even left Tunis."

There is so much to say and so much to tell about this very rich rendering of one's own interesting journey. From listening and learning, Mounira Chaieb is now a free-lancer training young journalists how to pass on the message of objectivity, accuracy, credibility, fairness, balance and above all real passion.

Mounira Chaieb's interaction with her two daughters about their growing up and realisation of racial and cultural belonging is full of lessons.

Had she not found a title for her book, I would have suggested: "The Voice of the Voiceless," or "God is Not a Hairdresser." Read the book and you will know why.

Ali Chokri, PhD Linguist & Media Analyst

I have known Mounira Chaieb for many ways as a gifted BBC colleague and a beautiful human being, and we even took an unforgettable reporting trip to Oman together; yet her book has taught me so much more about her roots in Tunisia and the perspective she brought to living and working in London.

It's a little gem of a read, not just for her friends. I warmly recommend it.

Kristine Pommert, Former BBC Executive Producer and current Head of CTVC Radio, London

I had a funny and beautiful relationship with the author and her late husband, the late Dr Tajudeen Abdul-Raheem. We shared intimacy and jokes.

On one occasion Tajudeen called from Southern Italy announcing with victory that he had purchased a brand - new video recorder at a very reasonable price to record his wife and myself. This was before the time of smart phones. Interestingly for him, the fancy recorder turned into a bag salt on the train back to Rome. He was 419ed as Nigerians say (meaning cheated) by a dodgy Italian guy in the back streets of Naples! How an Italian petty criminal with a visible scar across his face, could sell salt to the Oxford educated Nigerian was a subject of many jokes between the three of us.

After Mounira's and Tajudeen's traditional wedding ceremony in Tunis in August 1994 attended by Prof Abdul-Rahman Mohamed Babu (former Planning minister of the Republic of Tanzania), John Kayode Fayemi (Governor of Etiki State, Nigeria), myself among others, we drove to Libya to spend a few days. By the time we reached Tripoli, my suitcase was missing. Our 'in – laws' had taken it leaving me with nothing. This, however, did not deter me from appreciating the beauty of North Africa when we flew back over the beautiful island of Djerba, called the 'Dream Island' off the South Eastern coast of Tunisia.

On a more serious note, Mounira Chaieb's semi - autobiography of a bold journalist from Tunisia married to a popular Pan Africanist from Nigeria, told through dozens of anecdotes through lenses of the respected BBC World Service at Bush House (Central London) and across her travels around the globe offers a beautiful, formidably informative and readable story that touches on serious issues such as identity in the multicultural world.

Beautifully written, this book is a must read in understanding cross cultural challenges.

Napoleon Abdulai, Ghana's Ambassador to Cuba with concurrent accreditation to countries in the Caribbean and South America

Mounira Chaieb's account of her journey as a curious but sheltered young woman in Tunisia to the world of the BBC in London provides insights into the potential of the media to transform conditions around us.

It's a journey that begins thanks to Tunisia's radical policies under President Bourguiba to end gender discrimination – policies that set her apart from her own mother, who had no access to education. Chaieb walks us through some sensitive and delicate realities faced in her new life as a reporter – prejudice by Egyptians against their Sudanese neighbours, racial profiling and hostility towards North Africans in France. She describes how her Nigerian-born husband-to-be, the pan-Africanist icon Tajudeen Abdul-Raheem, through the sheer force of his personality overcomes family resistance to their marriage, given the context of anti-black prejudice in the Arab world and the Maghreb, and what she did to inculcate black pride in their daughters Aida and Ayesha after Aida's innocent 'but God is not a hairdresser!' nursery schoolkid remark.

There is also the satisfaction she experiences when a series of documentaries on disability results in the introduction by King Mohammed VI of Morocco of new laws giving people with disabilities job quotas in the public sector. She reveals the joy it is possible to feel as a journalist talking to "real people about real issues", amplifying the voice of the voiceless and turning her conviction into ground-breaking radio programmes.

The story she tells is full of rich anecdotes that can help inform social inclusion initiatives across Africa and beyond. It's a lovely read and I highly recommend it.

Dede Amanor-Wilks, journalist and development specialist

Printed in the United States
by Baker & Taylor Publisher Services